This book belongs to

....

Kids' Mini Psalm Book Series

I Am Confident In God and Fearless: Psalm 27

by Tayo Oshaye

Illustrated by Yana Popova

Acknowledgments

Special thanks to Ronnie Chapman, Darren Pinto, Mrs Funmi Ayodele, my sweetheart Michael and Yana Popova. Your various contributions made a big difference in this book. Thanks to Mary Kole for the editorial. Thanks to my pastors for inspiring me.
I give all the glory and praises to the Mighty God for His wonderful word.

"I am Confident in God and Fearless" (Psalm 27).

• • • • • • • • • • • •

Written by Tayo Oshaye

All rights reserved. No part of this publication may be used or reproduced by any means without the prior written permission of the author.
Text Copyright © 2018 Tayo Oshaye
Illustrations Copyright © 2018 Yana Popova a.k.a. YaPpy
Book design by Yana Popova a.k.a. YaPpy

• • • • • • • • • • • •

First Edition
ISBN 978-1-9993736-1-0 (soft cover)
ISBN 978-1-9993736-0-3 (e-book)

Published by:

Tayo Oshaye Publishing
Aberdeen, Scotland, United Kingdom
www.justkidsmadeinjesuschrist.com

Printed in the UK

This book is a work of non-fiction. It is an adaptation of Chapter 27 in the Book of Psalms. Unless otherwise indicated, scriptures quoted from the Holy Bible, International Children's Bible, copyright © 1986, 1988, 1999, 2015 by Tommy Nelson. Used by permission. (https://www.bible.com/bible/1359/PSA.27.1-14)
Hymnal songs are from public domain.

For more information regarding this book, please contact Tayo Oshaye:
Facebook/tayooshaye
Twitter/aa2shine
Publication rev. date: 12/10/2018

Prologue

Be strong and courageous. Do not be afraid or terrified because of them, for the Lord your God goes with you; He will never leave you nor forsake you . . . Do not be discouraged.

1. Onward, Christian soldiers!
Marching as to war,
With the cross of Jesus going on before.
Christ, the royal Master,
Leads against the foe;
Forward into battle,
See, His banners go!

Onward, Christian soldiers! Marching as to war,
With the cross of Jesus going on before.

2. At the sign of triumph
Satan's legions flee;
On then, Christian soldiers, on to victory!
Hell's foundations quiver
At the shout of praise:
Brothers, lift your voices,
Loud your anthems raise!

- Text by Sabine Baring-Gould (1834–1924)
- Music by Arthur S. Sullivan (1842–1900)
- A public domain hymn

Scripture references: Deuteronomy 31:6–8, Exodus 13:21–22

**The Lord is my light and the one who saves me. So why should I fear anyone? The Lord protects my life. So why should I be afraid?
— Psalm 27:1**

In the ocean, there lives a little happy dolphin named Chelsea. She loves to play with her friends, Neon the rainbow fish and Jemma the jellyfish.

Every morning, the sun comes up making even the deepest parts of the ocean bright! The sun amazes Chelsea, Neon, and Jemma. It helps them see many beautiful things as they swim about the big blue ocean.

Sometimes, Chelsea will jump out of the water! There she sees the seagulls flying and the penguins waddling.

"Fantastic, Chelsea!" said Neon and Jemma. Can you hear Chelsea click and whistle with excitement? Chelsea isn't afraid of the deepest part of the ocean or even the sharks or the bigger fish.

Evil people may try to destroy my body. My enemies and those who hate me attack me. But they are overwhelmed and defeated.
            — **Psalm 27:2**

One sunny day, Chelsea goes out to see Neon and Jemma. She clicked, whistled, and bustled happily as she swam. She heard some rumbling noises coming from behind a rock.

Rickety, swish . . . rickety, swish.

"Fur seals, wow!" said Chelsea. They were Rodd and Keilan — very troublesome "water rats," as they like to be called! The last time they met, they tore Chelsea's music notes.

Rodd said, "You again? We don't like to hear your voice around here."

With a suspicious look, Chelsea asked, "What do you want from me?"

Then Keilan yelled, "Get away from here, or we'll tear you apart!"

"Go someplace else to make your sounds," said Rodd and Keilan. Chelsea slowly moved away. Her eyes turned red.
"Huh!"

If an army surrounds me, I will not be afraid. If war breaks out, I will trust the Lord.
— Psalm 27:3

The mean fur seals came after Chelsea. The silly red crabs were with them cheering, "Hail, the water rats . . . the meanest in town!"

Chelsea had her bag of cupcakes and a tasty pie. Rodd came close, dragging Chelsea's bag.

"What do we have here?" Keilan sniffed. "Yummy, yummy, our lunch is here."

Chelsea wouldn't let go of her bag.

"Hey, let's see who wins! Hope we get some crumbs as well," clattered the naughty crabs.

"Stop it!" she cried, and her flukes went *flip-flap, flip-flap!* She moved forward and burst out, "Stop being mean. None of your threats bother me, and I won't let you have my —"

Before she finished speaking, the fur seals and the crabs fled! Chelsea's outburst had alerted the ocean patrol, led by Inspector Whiteshark.

"Are you all right?" asked Whiteshark as he swam behind Chelsea. Just in time.

"Phew, I'm all right. Thanks," replied Chelsea. "That was awful!"

> I ask only one thing from the Lord. This is what I want: Let me live in the Lord's house all my life. Let me see the Lord's beauty. Let me look around in his Temple.
> — Psalm 27:4

Now that the fur seals were out of the way, Chelsea swam merrily off to meet her friends! They were in the church.

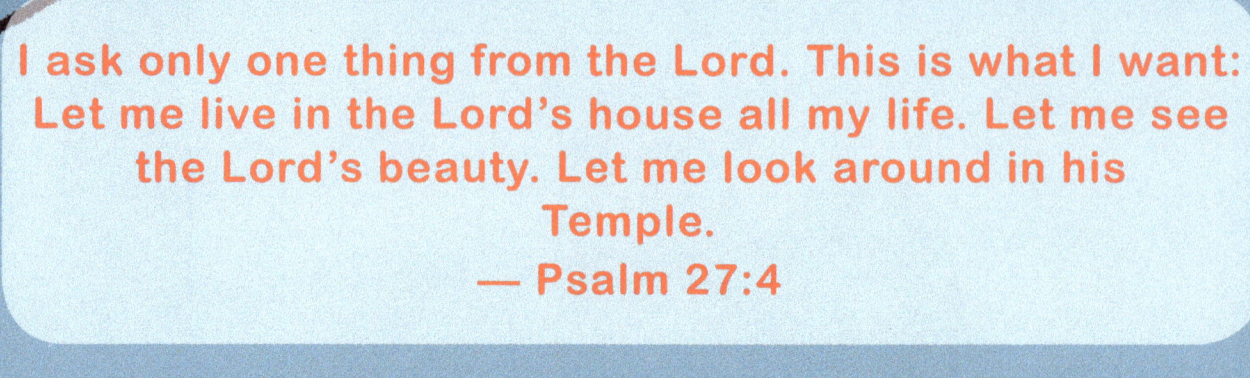

It's going to be a great day. I can't wait to get to the church. It's awesome how the choir sings, and I love the hymns too. I can stay there all day just to hear the amazing Bible stories at Sunday school.

Chelsea quietly entered the church. "Good morning, Neon."

"Good morning, Chelsea."

During danger, He will keep me safe in His shelter. He will hide me in His Holy Tent, or He will keep me safe on a high mountain.
—Psalm 27:5

Mia the minister told Chelsea's favourite story from the Bible, all about Joshua, the famous captain who led the Lord's Army.

She talked about how God keeps His people safe from danger. Chelsea smiled.

The next time the fur seals take my food or are mean to me, I will stand up to them. I will not fear them. God is with me. He will protect me from any harm.

> **My head is higher than my enemies around me. I will offer joyful sacrifices in his Holy Tent. I will sing and praise the Lord.**
> **— Psalm 27:6**

She then whispered a prayer: "God, I pray that Rodd and Keilan will stop being unkind to others. But thank you for my mum and dad, who care for me.

Thank you for my friends that I play with. Thank you for Mia the minister, and for all the good people in this big wide ocean."

At the end of the service, the church sang a lovely song, "The Lord is my Light and my Salvation; whom shall I fear?"

After church, off Chelsea went through the ocean.

Lord, hear me when I call. Be kind and answer me. My heart said of you, "Go, worship him." So I come to worship you, Lord.
— Psalm 27:7-8

On her way, she said, "If Rodd and Keilan will only be nice to everyone, this will be the best ocean ever."

She thought about the love of God. God is good and kind.

Every time my heart worships God, He blesses me. He hears me each time I pray. Because He is always kind, He will answer me.

Do not turn away from me. Do not turn your servant away in anger. You have helped me. Do not push me away or leave me alone, God, my Saviour. If my father and mother leave me, the Lord will take me in.
— Psalm 27:9-10

One day, Chelsea was practising her music lessons. Her mum came to her. Looking sad, she said, "Chelsea, your dad's job contract has expired."

"Oh dear!"

"We will be stopping your music classes because they're expensive."

"I'm sorry to hear what has happened to Dad." Chelsea was sad. She thought, *Why, Daddy?*

"We hope everything will be all right, hon."

Chelsea cried.

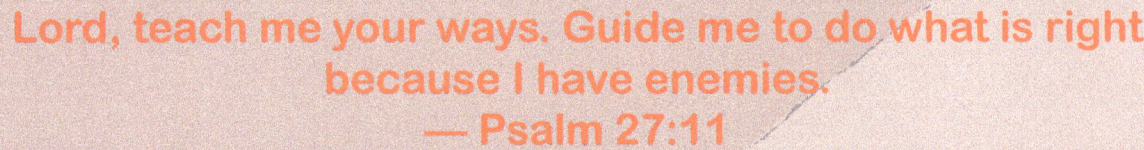

Lord, teach me your ways. Guide me to do what is right because I have enemies.
— Psalm 27:11

Feeling helpless, she knelt down by her bedside and prayed, "Oh, God, provide a new job for Dad, and let me be able to continue my music lessons. You have always looked after me. Lord, let me always be close to You. I will trust in You."

Chelsea pulled out her Bible and quietly flipped through the pages. She read about the little boy David who defeated the giant Goliath. "Hmm!" she said.

"I need God's wisdom. I will say yes to what is true. I will choose right with God's help. No matter what I face, I will do what is good in God's ways."

Do not let my enemies defeat me. They tell lies about me. They say they will hurt me.
— Psalm 27:12

The next time Chelsea met the fur seals, she was chanting, "This little light of mine."

Rodd and Keilan snarled. "Go away from here. What makes you think you can sing? Someone should've told you how horrible you sound."

Chelsea paused for a moment. "Hey! You don't have to be unkind. You may not like who I am. That is your problem. But I won't let your actions hurt my feelings."

The fur seals were quiet. They hid behind an ocean plant in shame. They never disturbed Chelsea again.

Neon was very thrilled about Chelsea's meeting with the fur seals. "Wow, that was brave, Chelsea! You were fearless!"

"Thank you, Neon. I had to be strong and courageous. God helped me overcome them."

When Chelsea got back home, her mum called. "Good news, Chelsea! Your dad got a new job closer to home, and we can continue your music lessons."

Click, click!

She thought, *I'm glad that I found my place in God. No matter what, I will never give up trusting in Him.*

www.ingramcontent.com/pod-product-compliance
Lightning Source LLC
Chambersburg PA
CBHW041234240426
43673CB00010B/333